FUN AND EAS

T0055802

arranged by John Cacavas

HAL LEONARD SOLO & ENSEMBLE SERIES

ISBN 978-1-4803-4527-0

HAL•LEONARD® CORPORATION

7777 W. BLUEMOUND RD. P.O. BOX 13819 MILWAUKEE, WI 53213

Visit Hal Leonard Online at
www.halleonard.com

WAVES OF THE DANUBE

IOSIF IVANOVICI

Arranged by JOHN CACAVAS

AULD LANG SYNE

TRADITIONAL SCOTTISH MELODY
Arranged by JOHN CACAVAS

04003394

GERMAN DANCE

FRANZ JOSEF HAYDN
Arranged by JOHN CACAVAS

THE RED RIVER VALLEY

TRADITIONAL COWBOY SONG
Arranged by JOHN CACAVAS

Copyright © 2013 by HAL LEONARD CORPORATION
International Copyright Secured   All Rights Reserved

TURKEY IN THE STRAW

AMERICAN FOLK SONG
Arranged by JOHN CACAVAS

AMERICA
(My Country, 'Tis of Thee)

from THESAURUS MUSICUS
Arranged by JOHN CACAVAS

04003394

POP GOES THE WEASEL

TRADITIONAL
Arranged by JOHN CACAVAS

HARK! THE HERALD ANGELS SING

FELIX MENDELSSOHN-BARTHOLDY
Arranged by JOHN CACAVAS

HOME ON THE RANGE

DANIEL E. KELLEY
Arranged by JOHN CACAVAS

DECK THE HALL

TRADITIONAL WELSH CAROL
Arranged by JOHN CACAVAS

04003394

MINUET NO. 1

(from *Notebook for Anna Magdalena Bach*)

J. S. BACH

Arranged by JOHN CACAVAS

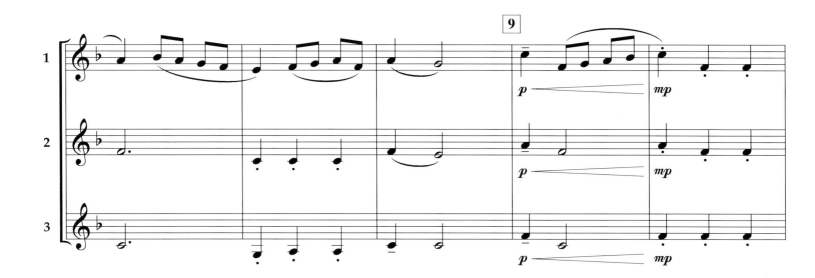

LONESOME ROAD

AFRICAN-AMERICAN SPIRITUAL
Arranged by JOHN CACAVAS

04003394

OLD FRENCH SONG

Op. 39, No. 16

P. I. TCHAIKOVSKY

Arranged by JOHN CACAVAS

O SOLE MIO

EDUARDO di CAPUA
Arranged by JOHN CACAVAS

ALL THROUGH THE NIGHT

WELSH FOLK SONG
Arranged by JOHN CACAVAS

SANTA LUCIA

ITALIAN FOLK MELODY
Arranged by JOHN CACAVAS

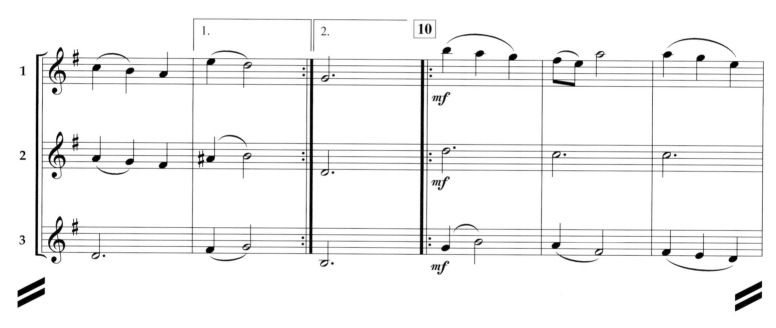

SWEET AND LOW

JOSEPH BARNBY
Arranged by JOHN CACAVAS

04003394

GOOD KING WENCESLAS

from PIAE CANTIONES
Arranged by JOHN CACAVAS

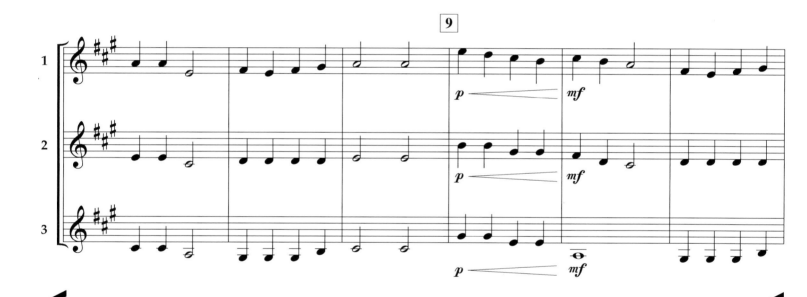

04003394

Copyright © 2013 by HAL LEONARD CORPORATION
International Copyright Secured   All Rights Reserved

CHORALE
from *St. Matthew Passion*

J.S. BACH
Arranged by JOHN CACAVAS

04003394

COUNTRY GARDENS

TRADITIONAL
Arranged by JOHN CACAVAS

HYMN

J. S. BACH
Arranged by JOHN CACAVAS

04003394

POEME

ZDENEK FIBICH
Arranged by JOHN CACAVAS